The
**Maxwell
Group**
Publisher

The RV Lifestyle Collection

For Women Only

Traveling Solo in Your RV

The Adventure of a Lifetime

Margo Armstrong

**For Women Only – Traveling Solo in Your RV
The Adventure of a Lifetime**

ISBN: 978-0692676264

 # From the Author

After traveling for many years with a partner in our 40-foot motorhome, I thought switching to solo might be a bit overwhelming. I relied totally on my partner to handle all the motorhome maintenance.

This meant learning new skills. Guess what, it turned out to be an easy transition even for me, not a mechanically in-clined individual.

Since many of my readers are women new to the RV life-style, I decided to write *For Women Only: Traveling Solo* for you. Included are all the details necessary to get you on the road right away.

If you are like me, an overview of how things work makes all the difference.

For Women Only: Traveling Solo In Your RV steps through all the basic requirements with plenty of photos.

After a few weeks on the road you become comfortable with the freedom, the lifestyle, and the joy of doing it on your own, like a pro.

Happy travels,

Margo Armstrong

Other Books by Margo Armstrong

Available at Online Bookstores Worldwide

RV LIFESTYLE COLLECTION

* *How To Save Money While Enjoying The RV Lifestyle*
* *The RV Lifestyle - A Dream Come True*
* *Selling Online - Supporting the Traveling Lifestyle*
* *Staying In Touch, A Traveler's Guide*
* *For Women Only - Traveling Solo In Your RV, The Adventure of a Lifetime*
* *For Women Only – Motorhome Care & Maintenance*
* *Working On The Road - For Professionals and Just Fun-Loving Folks*
* Conquer the Road – RV Maintenance for Travelers
* Healthcare & The RV Lifestyle

TOOLS FOR LIVING
* *Get Amazing Photos From Your Point & Shoot Camera*
* *Buying and Selling Gold and Silver - A Primer for the Beginning Investor*
* *Selling Your Home - How the Real Estate Market Works*
* *Do Your Own Probate - Summary Administration for Small Estates*

...More

Contents

Introduction

So, you have decided to turn your life into an adventure rather than living a life that seems destined to be empty. You are looking for new faces, new places, and joy. Even if your surroundings are filled with friends, family, and the same old events, you feel as though your life has come to a dead-end.

Now is the time to change all that. Pack up and go RVing. If you can escape for a few weeks, a few months, or full-time, do it.

After spending 20 years full-time in a motorhome, especially the last five years traveling solo, I have discovered a peace and security never felt before. The feeling of power and contentment from managing my own world grows with each passing day.

You are asking yourself at this moment if the voyage is right for you. Is it too much of a struggle? Can you really handle the mechanics of a large vehicle? Is driving this same behemoth within your capabilities? I do not have the answer for you but I can tell you that it is easier than it seems right now. Be open for adventure and tomorrow is always brighter.

Yes, it is scary at first. That is part of the experience and the excitement of mastering something you thought beyond your capabilities. It may not make the choice easier for you, but I can tell you that there are at least 20,000 women out there on the road today living the dream.

Today it seems scarier to me to think of driving a school bus on a busy city street than driving a motorhome down the highway. The average school bus is about the same size and we see women driving them all the time.

It is helpful to take a driver's training class before starting on your journey. There are several of these events happening all over the country, some specifically designed for women. This could be your first trip traveling to that class.

Maintenance classes, held every year by several RV clubs, are not necessary to get started. In fact, it helps if you have been traveling in your motorhome for at least a few weeks before taking a basic maintenance class.

Think about all the things you have done in the past to maintain your living space. How hard could maintaining a motorhome be in comparison?

Think about how little cleaning would be necessary. That alone should get you on the road. Kitchens in a motorhome are fully equipped and you can add what little extra you need to feel at home.

If cooking on a propane stove makes you uncomfortable, bring along an electric hotplate. Besides, cooking for yourself is easy and simple anyway.

The toilet works differently and there is a little bit to learn about it (see *Tips For A Happy Toilet*).

Forget about engine maintenance; let this be handled by an expert in whatever location you find yourself. You already know how to check the water and oil because you do this on the car you drive every day.

If you always have someone else handle those duties, do the same for the motorhome. Nearly every RV park has recommendations for local mechanics.

One last thought...most men I have met on the road know less than I do about their motorhome. Do not let them intimidate you. Take all their advice and put it aside, then call an experienced repairperson (or better yet, search the Internet first for the basic info).

The more you know the better skill you have for selecting the right person to fix or maintain your motorhome.

The RVing community is large and helpful. Help is out there just as it is for the house you live in (or used to live in).

It might be wise to take this full-time RVing aptitude test to see if this is the lifestyle for you.

ftrv.com/ftrvtest.html

Visit the *RVing Women* website and join an excellent support group for women only. They offer classes, rallies, and friendship. **www.rvingwomen.com**

Everything you need to know right now is contained in *For Women Only: Traveling Solo in Your RV*.

▶ *Letting Go of the Fear - Safety on the Road*
▶ *Breaking the News to Your Family*
▶ *Basics of Buying An RV*
▶ *Important Features When Buying*
▶ *Choosing a Home Base*
▶ *Buying an RV Long Distance*
▶ *Tips on Maintaining an RV*
▶ *Staying In Touch with Family and Friends*
▶ *Making New Friends and Having Fun*
▶ *Finding the Best Choices in RV Accommodations*
▶ *Supplementing Your Income While Traveling*

Safety on the Road

Before you can decide if the RV lifestyle is the right choice for you, you need to feel safe about traveling alone. Ignore all the negative thoughts and stories you hear about women traveling alone. It is all about common sense.

▶ Before starting on your first trip, send the time and money to have the following areas serviced at a local RV specialist shop:

- Oil change (consider using at least part synthetic oil)
- Transmission service
- Differential service (if applicable)
- Brake lining and brake shoes (if applicable)
- Tire pressure and condition (have the technician write down the manufacturer's date)
- Air filter (important for diesel engines)
- Correct amount of coolant in radiator (ask if the temperature sensor is working and correct)

▶ Choose your overnight accommodations wisely; more on this in the *"Finding the Best Choices"* chapter.

▶ Make sure you have a road service membership before you leave home.

▶ Travel with a small dog if it makes you feel more comfortable. Another choice is to carry one of those electronic toys that bark.

► Never open your door to strangers. Always keep your deadbolt locked. I open one of my front windows first until I identify the person. At night, I always turn on the porch light first, then open the window.

► Avoid traveling at night. Schedule your plans so by late afternoon you are in your overnight spot. Remember, we are not in a hurry.

► Avoid boondocking (staying overnight in places with no hookups) unless you are meeting friends or a group of RV colleagues.

► Ensure your fire extinguishers are updated, just in case. In all the years I have spent on the road, I have yet to see a motorhome on fire.

►Keep several types of flashlights handy. I keep a *Energizer Weather Ready* lantern near the door in case I need to check something outside at night.

Its slim design and bright LED lights are almost bright enough to be seen from space. It also has a muted light option for stealthy missions, like taking your beloved pet for a necessary walk after dark.

That is about it, not much to know. No one can break in through the windows because they are too high. Keep in mind, you are always surrounded by other RVers, hopefully not too close <grin>.

RVers watch out for each other, so if it is a community of strangers when you arrive, it may not be for long.

After the first few weeks in your motorhome, the security blanket becomes obvious and comfortable. As a friend of mine often remarks, "*You are wrapped in your cocoon, protected from the world.*"

Keep in mind that help is always close at hand. If you spend the time to find the motorhome that is right for you, and keep it maintained, any small problems that arise after you have reached your destination can be handled by someone in the RV park. You can also have an outside vendor come directly to you.

Notes:

Breaking the News to Your Family

If you have never owned an RV and taken your family on a trip, they are naturally concerned about your new adventure. If your family is close, invite them over for the day. You might stay a night in a local RV park to check everything out. Invite the family over the next day to have a look around. Make it a celebration!

In an interesting conversation with the grown daughter of one of my RV neighbors, she voiced concerned about her mother traveling in a motorhome. Her vision of struggle and sacrifice persisted until she saw the inside of her mother's motorhome. She exclaimed in an excited voice, *"Mom has everything she needs. I had no idea."*

If your family is located too far away to visit, send them pictures of the outside and inside. Explain that almost every destination park has maintenance people on-hand to help or can recommend someone to take care of almost any issue that might arise.

Make sure your family has all your legal paperwork for emergency care, any health directives or other documents they might need. For the first year (maybe less), a telephone call when you arrive at your destination should put aside any fears.

Children (of any age) rarely have a true picture of their own mother's capabilities. Let them know about the good times shared with new friends.

Keep the fact that you "forgot to dump the gray water before the shower backed up" to yourself (more about this later).

If your children call every day and beg you to come home, open a Facebook account. On your homepage, keep recent photos and travel notes there. Start a travel blog for free at:

- Wordpress.com
- Blogger.com
- Websitebuildertop10.com

Basics of Buying a Motorhome

You are probably wondering why I only mention motorhomes and not fifth wheels, trailers, pop-ups, or custom vans. Traveling solo for a season, or especially full-time, requires an adequate amount of space and convenience to make the lifestyle comfortable.

Of course, if you want to "try out" the lifestyle, a custom van works. You do not need any advice on that purchase; it is just a small truck. I do not recommend fifth wheels or trailers for solo travel due to the extra work and physical strength required in setting up for the night.

Motorhomes come in two classes; Class A and Class C. Many women choose the Class C due to the lower cost and the smaller size normally available. I prefer a Class A for better construction and interior layout.

Before you begin your wandering lifestyle, select the perfect RV. Right away, you save huge sums of money by deciding whether you want mobility or living space. Ask yourself the following questions:

▶ Do I want primarily to stay in state, county and city parks to explore the area, or prefer private or commercial parks?

▶ Do I want to stay in one location for the winter and another for the summer, or travel to a new location whenever I feel like it?

▶ Am I planning to live all year in my RV, or maintain my primary home and travel occasionally?

▶ Am I an adventurer or a nester?

▶ Do I want to live the same lifestyle I had in my house, or streamline my lifestyle to take advantage of mobility?

The answers to these questions dictate the length and layout of your first RV. If you follow the tips included here, the first motorhome purchase can enhance the RV experience, eliminate stress and build confidence.

Buy Quality

Ignore the glitter of brand new interiors and think of value versus the dollar spent.

▶Check the wall and cabinet construction on the inside. Ask about the quality of the insulation, type of suspension, roofing, braking system, engine, transmission, and other outside details. Do some basic Internet research on these areas.

▶Often the lower-priced motorhomes need after-market suspension and safety mechanisms added to make the driving experience acceptable.

▶Purchasing a used high-end motorhome gives you long term enjoyment and saves you the disappointment of a new purchase gone badly.

▶Let the original owner purchase all the after-market enhancements...and spend the time at the manufacturer repairing the glitches...allowing you to drive away with a highway-ready rig.

▶Spend as much time to find the right rig as you would to buy a house. Search the Internet and RV-related magazines for RV ads.

▶Join e-mail discussion groups where RV owners talk about their experience with different types of rigs. Ask for suggestions about what to buy, new and used.

▶Remember to explain that you are a woman traveling solo as this often moves the discussion down a different path.

▶Of course, as you already know, if is wise to avoid offering any personal information during these discussions other than your return E-mail address.

►When searching for the right used RV, pay attention to the original **new price**. This helps define whether it is high-quality rig or a possible nightmare.

►There are many models within a brand name, so do not assume they are all the same quality machines. Some manufacturers actually contract out the lower-priced models (no quality control).

►Once you have found a few models that meet your requirements, join a Yahoo group that discusses this brand. Sometimes reading a single message can point out a feature (or lack thereof) that is important to you.

►Almost all discussion groups have "search" tools. This can save lots of time and frustration. Try the model name first. If this does not bring up the desired results, try one feature, for instance, "diesel," "30 ft.," or "slides."

►Try to be as objective as possible when selecting the right RV. It is important to have a interior layout that works for you, but quality of construction and price may be more important.

►Since this is your first experience with an RV, keep in mind that having a huge living room (or salon) may not be as important as a bigger bathroom or kitchen space.

►Since most RVers spend much of their social time outdoors in camping chairs, or around a picnic table, indoor entertainment space is not a priority.

►However...If you intend to carry on with your bridge parties, then living room slideouts move to the top of the list; if you are a crafts person, then adequate storage rules.

►Price may ultimately dictate the final purchase. Since this is your first motorhome purchase, paying cash versus the cost of financing may also play a role in your decision.

►Keep in mind that some of the nicer parks that offer seasonal rates require the motorhome to be 10 years old or newer before they rent you the space.

►That said, older high-end coaches in good exterior condition are often admitted after inspection by the manager. Tip: If your coach has full body paint, acceptance is guaranteed.

►If you are looking for a pre-2001 used Class A high-end coach, Beaver, Country Coach, and Foretravel are among the most recognized high-end coaches. For a Class C, look at Lazy Daze and Born Free.

►Although today's manufacturers cannot compete with the outstanding exterior and interior construction of these earlier coaches, Monaco, Tiffin, Winnebago, Gulf Stream, Thor, and Holiday Rambler all provide a top-of-the-line model.

Get Started

Finding a used 25- to 33-foot length quality Class A coach is the more difficult task. In 2011, Itasca, Newmar and Thor all introduced new, smaller Class As in this length. These are all mid-quality construction but are well equipped, gas or diesel.

Search the Internet first for the Class A or the Class C layout that meets your needs. Write down the year, model, price, and layout designation of several motorhomes that meet your specifications. Visit these sites for comparisons.

- www.RVTrader.com
- www.rvonline.com
- www.pplmotorhomes.com

Next, start looking locally, using newspaper ads, Craigslist, and dealerships. Sometimes taking a tour of a particular model helps you decide if it meets your needs.

This is where dealer lots come in handy. *Just do not buy that one until you exhaust the for-sale-by-owner possibilities.*

I know, it takes courage to walk away from the motorhome that excites you. Keep in mind, you can usually save thousands of dollars by negotiating directly with the owner and probably purchase a better-maintained vehicle.

Owners usually have maintenance records they are proud to show you. Dealers, on the other hand, destroy all maintenance documentation before they display the vehicle. You get the point, "buyers beware."

A simple pre-purchase examination, at the very least, can give you a heads-up on this motorhome. It is also an opportunity to learn the basics of operation from the inspector.

Important Features

That Make the Lifestyle Work

▶ **Hydraulic Levelers**:

Without levelers built into the coach chassis: Placing wood or plastic blocks under the wheels at each overnight stop to level the coach becomes tiresome. Most refrigerators need to be level to work properly and to avoid expensive maintenance. In my opinion, this is the most important feature to look for.

▶ **Chassis safety options** to improve driving comfort and confidence:

Safe-T-Plus on the front end to ensure that if a tire blowout occurs, the coach can navigate safely to the side of the road. This also improves the ability to keep the coach riding in a straight line.

Track bar (or similar) to keep the rear end from swinging during highway speeds. This is especially important if towing a car.

▶ Ensure that the awning is encased in an aluminum shroud when closed for traveling. This eliminates the chance of losing the awning in high winds during travel.

▶ Look for as much storage as possible. Check basement storage, inside closet space, and inside overhead storage.

▶If **slide-outs** are important to you:

One thing to look for is the vertical stance of the slide as it moves in and out.

All slides have the same type of roller assembly at the outer wall but the slide should maintain its stability (with little tipping in or out) as it moves in and out.

Poor stability can damage the floor and can affect the slides ability to seal.

On new and used motorhomes, carefully inspect top and side seals. You need to understand how the seal is supposed to work, how it is working and the prospect of how long it continues to work after years of use.

If you are left shaking your head you do not want to buy this motorhome. Water, light, varmints, insects, etc. can get in if the slides are not properly sealed.

Pre- Purchase Checkout

Regardless of whether you purchase a Class A or a Class C motorhome, **always, always, always** have an independent RV mechanic checkout the vehicle before you sign on the dotted line. This process can save you a lot of headaches and money later.

Minimum pre-purchase examination checklist:

Air Conditioners (roof and engine-driven)
Awning
Batteries (test for life cycle)
Door lock
Engine
Hydraulic levelers
Propane system (test for leaks)
Roof coating and seals around vents, air conditioner, antennas
Slideout seals (if applicable)
Refrigerator
Water Heater
Window seals

Things you can check yourself:

Microwave
Window shades or blinds
Water flow
Toilet
Light fixtures

Some RV repair shops do not charge for this checkout service, hoping they can charge the owner to fix the items that wind up on their checklist. Other shops might charge $100 to spend the hour necessary. You may be able to negotiate with the owner to pay for the fixes, or drop the price.

If you purchase through an RV dealer (not recommended), this may be an issue to work out as one of their maintenance or sales people needs to drive the vehicle to the shop.

Always arrange to be there personally during the inspection. Do not skip this step no matter what tale the sales person spins. If they refuse to cooperate, walk away.

A friend of mine bought her first motorhome from a dealer who sold her this perfect motorhome at a great price. After two months and $8,000 worth of repairs, she returned it to the dealer and traded for a newer model.

Still she trusted this dealer to do the right thing. She drove off the lot with a much newer (and much more expensive) motorhome. Again, $3,000 worth of repairs before the motorhome could safely ply the roads again.

The point being that usually people trade in their motorhomes when they begin to suspect that they need to spend thousands of dollars on repairs.

Dealers take these vehicles in trade usually without regard to condition. The dealer's profit margin is so high on the newer motorhome they sold this customer, they can afford to do this on a trade.

If the exterior is presentable, they sell the trade to some unsuspecting newbie. How they sleep at night is beyond me.

This is similar to the way people look at their automobiles. If they really enjoy a vehicle, they continue to keep up the maintenance until it overwhelms them with repair costs. If it is junk to start with, they get rid of it sooner rather than later.

On the other hand, some people sell their motorhomes simply because they want a new feature, a new layout, a diesel rather than a gas engine. Some sell because of ill health. This is the type of motorhome you are looking for. If possible, buy your first motorhome from this owner.

Notes:

FSBO or Commercial RV Lot

As you have already figured out, finding the right RV is important. It is also a time of great excitement and emotional turmoil. The urge to grab an RV and hit the road is almost overwhelming, right? Now is the time to take a deep breath and let logic and intuition rule.

Also, know that over 50% of long term RVers change vehicles in the first five years of their travels. Important features are often overlooked until you experience owning one.

To get the right RV the first time, here are a few tips:

- Decide if you want to travel (motorhome) or stay several months in one location (fifth wheel). Forget about the extra space in a fifth wheel if you have to back it into a space and set up every few weeks.

- The first change RVers make is a switch from one type to the other. If you are a travel bug, do not consider trailers or fifth wheels, go motorhome.

- Without experience driving a big rig, start with something in the Class A motorhome 30-33 foot range, or Class C motorhome 24-28 foot range. If one of the drivers has experience, the best economic value is in a 10-year old 40-foot high-quality motorhome. Full body paint is important for the long-term look.

- The layout is important no matter the type, if you are planning to travel full-time. Slide-outs are a nice addition along with a washer/dryer. A microwave oven with convection option is a "must have" in my book.

- A important feature is storage space. Having full basement compartments, automatic levelers, and good tires are on the list too.

- Ensure that the salon is laid out to suit you, the TV in the right place, not too many sofas, etc. Resist the urge to redecorate until at least six months down the road; you cannot recoup the money spent if you decide to change vehicles later.

- Know that previously owned Class C models are built on a much cheaper chassis that the Class A, so construction is not as solid. If you buy new, look for quality Class Cs recently introduced into the marketplace since 2010, such as *Born Free*.

▶ Once the basic decision is made (motorhome or 5th-wheel), search RVT.com and RVTrader.com. Another valuable site to search is RVUSA.com.

▶ Choose three models you like. Write down (copy/paste into a text file) all the specifications for the RV, including the extras. Make sure the length and model number are included.

▶ Decide on a gas (much cheaper original cost) or a diesel (more power, longer life) engine to power it.

▶ Use the NADAGuides.com database to get a price range on each model.

▶ Read this excellent article about how much you should pay: www.rversonline.org/ArtFAQ3.html.

[You have followed the suggestions above, but the RV that looks like a perfect fit is not located near you. Read the *Buying an RV Long Distance* chapter.]

▶ Next, call the local RV dealers to see if they have these models (at least one of them) on their lot. If so, spend some time inside and carefully look at the interior, the appliances, how the walls meet the doors (if you see staples, cross this one off).

▶ Next, get serious about finding the one choice remaining on the list from a private owner. Here is a list of websites to peruse:

- RVOnline.com

- Escapees RVNetwork.com forum

- RVsFSBO.com

- RVUSA.com

- ClassyRV.com/

Always, always, always have an independent RV inspector check out the rig before signing on the dotted line. Use the NRVIA.com site to find a certified inspector. If unable to find a local inspector, RV repair shops are everywhere, and most have someone who can perform this service.

DO NOT SKIP THIS STEP. Have the current owner drive it to the facility (liability reasons), or hire a mobile RV repair-person/certified inspector. Now is the time to negotiate.

If you wind up at a dealer's lot (last choice), have a mobile service stop by for an hour. Always plan to attend this, never accept the salesperson's word. Be prepared to walk away if the dealer refuses the inspection by an independent service person.

Be careful with dealer warranties, do your research first. Do not assume anything while at the dealer's lot. Get everything in writing. Be prepared to deal with sales personalities; do not let them intimidate you.

Most people living the RV lifestyle tell you, if asked, what their first buying experience is like. I do not have stats, but I would guess that most people buy their first and last RV from a dealer. The reasons usually boil down to RV availability and local resources. This clearly explains the stats stated earlier about changing rigs within five years.

With few exceptions, RV dealers have a different set of ethics, similar to used car dealers, than what you expect. They want to sell the dream. If it turns out not to be your dream, buyer beware is the policy.

If the pricing sounds too good to be true, it probably is. Since you have done your research (see above), you know the current price range to expect. Step back and let the RV inspector finish the report. Somewhere along this path, the story may change.

If you are trading in an older model RV, or simply one that does not work for you, the trade-in value may be inflated to increase the retail on the new one. Just because there is a guarantee of satisfaction, even in writing, it does not state whose satisfaction rules.

It is the norm for dealers to remove all documentation from the RV. This may happen a thousand miles away or when traded in on another model. Dealers can then truthfully deny knowing anything about the rig.

Let me tell you one little story about a corporate executive friend of mine who decided to retire to an RV.

She bought her first rig from a dealer and it immediately started falling apart.

The dealer, of course, kindly accepted the rig back in trade on a newer model, giving my friend an outstanding trade-in value on the newer rig. What a great deal, she thought.

Then, the front door jammed shut and had to be removed by a mechanic. The front step stopped working, the awning arm needed replacing, and the list went on. This rig had obvious been in an accident that knocked everything out of balance. An inspector would have caught all of this.

The outside of both rigs looked in good condition. Neither rig was inspected before purchase. Fortunately, my friend, still in the shakedown phase, had not yet left town. The dealer was no longer supportive, surprise!

The experience left her shaken and morose. She sold the RV and banished the RV lifestyle from her life. She missed the experience of a lifetime.

Many stories like this one are available; but you get the picture. When you are spending this kind of money, why not spend another $250 for an inspector and know the health of the machine...before you buy it.

You might spend a little more ($41-$125) and have a fluids analysis done so you know the true health of the engine.

Is this same negative buying experience possible when purchasing from individuals?

Yes, it is, however, individuals usually have all the paperwork from past maintenance.

They are happy to walk you through everything they know about the rig. Once the inspection is completed, they either pay to have any repairs made, or lower the price.

All three of my motorhomes were purchased from individuals who no longer traveled. In addition, yes, the few problems we negotiated usually with a price drop.

Individuals that have the time and patience to sell their RVs, tend to take care of their rigs, so generally fewer problems exist.

To sum it all up, dealers do not interact with the RVs they sell. They take in trades from RV rental companies, vehicles from other lots that cannot sell them, and other venues.

Dealers rarely turn down a trade if the exterior is not damaged. Engine problems, appliance problems, suspension problems...they do not really care about that. They know someone new to the RV lifestyle can walk in and drive out with it.

They may know something about the brand, but absolutely no experience with this particular RV. Your purchase pays their mortgage; they need to sell you something. They are taught not to stimulate any questions.

RV dealer lots that have a high-volume turnover in vehicles may indeed have a trade-in that works for you.

There is no need to fear this process if the inspector gives it a clean slate (or at least problems you can deal with). You already know the price range so you can work with that.

Find out everything you can about the deal, then GO HOME. Give yourself at least 24 hours to decide if this deal works for you.

If you sense anything is out of order, move on. Your intuition is probably right. Keep your emotions in check.

You may need this purchase right now because your house is sold and the new owners want to move in right away. Since the pressure is on, make a list of the problems to be solved with the rig.

Negotiate the price down to where you can make the repairs privately and still be okay on the money. This type of research is where the Internet really sings. Spend some time here to save more money.

Buying an RV Long Distance

Find the Perfect RV

You have looked online and found several RVs that look promising as the "perfect" RV.

The layout looks good for you, the price range is right, it has hydraulic levelers, powerful enough diesel engine, big enough TV, quality built, enough slides, and includes most of what you wanted; it happens to be in Arizona, California, Utah ... pick a state.

Send An Inspector

A new organization is available to assist you, the *National RV Inspection Association*. They certify, and help you search for, RV inspectors. Go to **NRVIA.org** and use the search field to find an inspector in the area where the rig is located.

RVInspection. com is an inspection company comprised of NRVIA-certified personnel. Find out everything you need to know about what they include in their inspections. Pricing starts at $295 and includes photos. Take a look at the reports they generate or create your own list.

Have this inspector go look at the RV and send you a report. If it is the right RV, make a deal with the owner using the *Intent to Purchase* agreement found on the website.

You can drive there to pick the motorhome up or have it driven to you by a professional.

An *RV Purchase Option Agreement* is helpful to complete the deal. Use this example found on the website and create your own agreement, or use as is.

The RV could also be delivered to an RV driving school, meet it there, take the course and drive away. See "Driving-Schools-BootCamps" at **RVLifestyleExperts.com** for a list.

The RV inspector makes sure you do not get a lemon, so you cannot lose there. You might also want to get a fluid analysis to ensure the engine is in good condition. The inspector should be able to help you.

Believe me, the first RV sets the stage for a great experience. Get the right one for you. Having the RV inspected by a professional is always a good idea no matter where you buy it; even if the inspector is a local RV repair person right next door.

Transfer Funds

Transferring funds to the current owner of the RV you want to buy is tricky under the best of circumstances. Due to the large amounts of cash usually involved, security is the big issue. What if the owner is a thousand miles away?

If you use a wire transfer - bank to bank - what guarantees a safe arrival of the vehicle? The owner might agree to half down and half when you receive it. Still...we are talking large amounts of cash.

Most buyers rely on an escrow service to provide the security. If you are on friendly terms with your banker, that service might be available to you. If not, the only national escrow service in the USA that I am aware of is **Escrow.com**. Spend some time researching this solution.

Information from their website:

- Online escrow that is simple and safe for Buyers and Sellers

- A licensed and regulated escrow company compliant with Escrow Law

- Regularly audited by government authorities

Headquartered in Rancho Santa Margarita, California, *Escrow.com* is a privately held company that has pioneered the process of online escrow services. The Company, founded in 1999 by Fidelity National Financial, has established itself as one of the leading providers of secure business and consumer transaction management on the Internet.

Buying and selling vehicles online has never been easier or more secure. *Escrow.com's* simple 5-step process ensures money transfer and vehicle delivery with every sale.

To make your vehicle sale easier, they offer timesaving services, such as Lien Payoff and Title Collection; they also recommend companies who can provide vehicle transport.

Escrow service fees as low as 0.89% of the purchase price.

Note: the fee schedule is not straightforward. Based on the selling price in increments, the higher the amount transferred, the lower the overall fee.

For example: Purchase a fifth wheel for $20,000; pay an escrow fee of around $200. Buyer or Seller (or Broker if applicable) can pay this fee, or split between them. Read the details carefully.

Ship the RV to You

The most popular shipping company for recreational vehicles in the USA is UShip.com. This company is really a network of drivers that bid on your project. It can be entertaining to watch the drivers try to underbid each other.

You can get sample quotes on this website if you want to check the pricing without starting a price war.

Some information from their website:

Transporting your RV with *uShip* is the best way to get it wherever it needs to go. Maybe you need somebody to drive your RV to its destination, or maybe you would like to save the mileage on your RV and have it transported on a trailer. Whichever method or carrier you choose, it can be simple and affordable to have your RV transported. That way, you can get back on the road making memories and living in your second home.

RV Transport may appear to be a complicated process, but in most cases it is as easy as shipping any other kind of auto transport.

By allowing a few weeks to choose a transporter, make arrangements, and prepare your RV for transport, you can be sure that the entire process goes smoothly.

When transporting an RV, consider important issues such as proper licensing, RV insurance coverage, and turnaround time, Ask questions until you are satisfied.

You can request a RV transporter to tow or drive your RV, depending on what type or classification it is.

Preparing an RV for transport does not take long, but it is important, because RVs are complex vehicles that could be damaged during transport. A categorized checklist is useful for preparation.

Finally, before handing off your RV to a transporter, you should check that your RV is covered in case of an accident or damage. This is as simple as asking about RV transport insurance and checking RV transporter qualifications against public records.

Understanding an RV shipping contract and insurance issues protects you in case of an accident.

Once you find the perfect RV make and interior layout, use the following resources to check for value and quality.

Choosing the First RV - Resources

RV Consumer Group: This group analyzes RV brands and manufacturers in the following way: Consumer surveys, staff evaluations, visiting dealer lots, attending RV shows, and making unannounced visits to RV factories.

They review the type of consumer complaint against a brand and compare it to the input received through surveys and staff evaluations.

RV Guide: If you are in the market for an RV, be sure to take a look at some of these reviews before you make your final decision. RV Guide puts each of its test units through its paces and tells you exactly what to expect, what works, and what does not.

RV Reviews: RV Reviews offers the most comprehensive RV Consumer Buying Guides on the internet. Find your new or used RV with non-biased recommendations and expert advice. Their RV buying guides help you select the best RV model and save thousands in the process. They rate over 105 RV manufacturers in North America and provide individual model ratings.

NADA Guides: These guides are free to research new and used recreation vehicle pricing, specs, photos, and special options for everything from travel trailers to truck campers.

NADA Guides offer a broad range of data, products and services, informational articles, tips, advice and video buying guides that help make the vehicle purchasing process easier for consumers.

In addition to being the leading provider of vehicle pricing and services to consumers, NADA Guides is also the largest provider of vehicle data and information to the nation's leading banks, credit unions, fleet and lease organizations, dealers, insurance companies, government agencies and financial institutions.

Make and Model Forums on the Internet usually discuss one brand and related models. These individual forums focus on real-time issues and may answer real-time questions for you.

As an example, if you are undecided about whether to purchase the gas or diesel model, search the forum for an answer or join the forum to ask the question. Search term: (make & model + forum) e.g., Safari Trek forum.

Financing Costs

The most expensive part of owning an RV is the cost of financing it. As the market value of a new RV drops 40 to 50% after the first day of ownership, be prepared to pay more in interest than the vehicle is worth at the end of the finance contract. The market value continues to drop with each passing year just like any vehicle.

Used high-end coaches, on the other hand, can be financed like new ones and depreciate much slower.

Extended Warranties

Most after-market warranties prove to be disappointing when you try to collect. If you feel more secure purchasing one, pay for only one year. If you are full-timing or seasonal-living in your RV, any major problem should emerge within that timeframe.

Dealing with the Repair Shop

With all the horror stories floating around about the RV repair business, who can you trust to take care of major repairs or install add-ons to personalize your motorhome.

▶ Ask at the RV park front desk for reliable services that guests have recommended.

▶ Always ask for a written work order with the repairs or services written down and a cost estimate explained in detail.

Have them place *right on the work order* that any extra costs over $100 requires a phone call and approval from you **before** any work is performed.

Ensure that you walk away with a copy of the work order.

▶ Do not hesitate to discuss the final bill with the shop owner if you have a problem with it.

▶ If the shop refuses to follow your guidelines, find another vendor.

▶ Woodworking and cabinetmaking is the most expensive and frustrating project of them all. Finding a quality craftsman that can fulfill your dream is difficult.

Keep looking until you get a referral from someone that actually has personal experience with the crafts person or persons.

Sales Tax and Registration Fees

Before you buy that RV, spend some time thinking about taxes and fees. You may want to have the new or used rig delivered for you to pick up in a state other than the one in which you currently reside. Some states have no sales tax; others have high taxes.

If you are buying a used vehicle, think about buying in one of the states that offer a tax advantage.

▶ Remember, you must have an reliable street address within the state for license renewal notices, drivers license, and insurance paperwork.

▶ Search the Internet for information on states that currently offer full-timers a safe haven. Look for low registration fees and state taxes.

▶ Several states cater to the RV owner. They offer low registration fees and no sales tax on the purchase price.

Note: Some states, like Arizona, do not charge sales tax when purchasing directly from the owner. Sales tax only applies when purchasing from a dealer.

Preferred States

For the unofficial Guide to motor vehicle requirements, visit **dmv.org** for basic information on all 50 states. This private website provides links to official motor vehicle offices and offers free information.

▶**Oregon** - No sales tax but does have state income tax.

- License fees are based on the length of the vehicle and valid for two years. Oregon has strict residency requirements for registration. This is the result of California and Washington applying pressure because of the low fees.

- Here is a link to official Oregon RV information. **Oregon.gov**

▶ **Montana** - No sales tax on RV purchases or personal property tax.

- Residency requirements are avoided by creating an LLC.

- Visit **www.rvconsulting.com/** for a basic FAQ about the LLC process.

▶ **South Dakota** - No state inheritance tax, no personal property tax, no intangible tax on investments. [Medical insurance may be a problem when traveling, as South Dakota pre-Medicare programs only cover in-state claims.]

- 3% excise tax on purchase of RVs and other vehicles

- Low vehicle licensing fee

- Ranks 47th in lowest private passenger car insurance rates

▶**Texas** – No State Income Tax, RV-friendly, but annual equipment check required.

- License fees based on GVW.

- Registration is reasonable but insurance is higher than the other states mentioned here.

▶**Florida** – Because of medical insurance issues for full-timers under 65, this state is added to the preferred list, replacing South Dakota for the younger crowd.

- No state income tax, sales tax runs 6-9.5%, licensing is by weight, not the length or age.

- Auto insurance may be higher than other states, so do your research before committing.

For detailed home base information on all 48 states, visit: **www.rv-travel-with-kids.com/50-states-facts.html**

Emergency Road Service

Courtesy of Good Sam

Do not leave home without emergency road service. Check your RV insurance policy to make sure this is included. Call and discuss this coverage with your agent.

Several independent emergency road service companies offer more options. Listed here are only a few of the available services.

www.nmc.com - Coach-Net Unlimited RV Road Service (recommended)

www.goodsamers.com - Good Sam Road Service

www.aaa.com - Triple A Road Service

To be financially prepared in case of a road emergency, ask yourself (and your insurance agent), these questions:

Are all towing charges covered?

Is there a limit to the number of miles my RV can be towed?

Is there a dollar limit on the coverage?

Is trip delay insurance provided in case of a collision? What is the dollar amount?

Is the question of vehicle safety taken into consideration on any limitations?

How long does it take to connect to the service before receiving assistance?

Any guarantees on the speed of assistance?

Is assistance available 24x7?

If there is a deductible, when exactly does it apply?

Any fee discounts available if I have a certain make and model of RV?

Is my car or truck covered?

Notes:

Motorhome Maintenance Tips

Gas or Diesel

Mileage per gallon (mpg) is relatively the same, with diesel coming out ahead by 1 or 2 miles per gallon (7-8 mpg) more than gas (4-6 mpg) when comparing used motorhomes. The new motorhomes rate considerable better in both engine types. However, you can buy a lot of gas or diesel with the money saved by buying used.

The question to ponder is "do I want a diesel engine for power and long life...or a gas engine for up-front savings and ease of maintenance?"

Diesel Engines

Diesel engines with their long life span, greater power, and better fuel economy seem to be popular in the new motorhome market. As diesel engines are generally an unknown quantity to first-time RVers, research the different manufacturers before buying. The low-end Detroit engine appears in many new coaches. The Caterpillar and Cummins engines are found in the higher quality rigs. The horsepower varies from 250 to 450+.

The difference in price for diesel engine motorhomes is several thousand dollars from the low-end to the high-end, even in used rigs. Quality pays off here again. Repairs on these engines run into thousands of dollars.

They also go 350,000 miles without a glitch. Maintenance, as with all types of engines, must be kept up-to-date. Filters must be monitored as dirty ones easily foul the engine. Attention to detail makes the difference between flawless performance and costly repairs.

Gas Engines

Gas engines, on the other hand, cut the cost of a new vehicle by $20,000 or more. In used vehicles, however, gas engines may be close to end-of-life. These engines are more familiar to the average owner and maintenance along with the cost of repair is lower. It may be wise to have the oil tested when you have the inspector stop by.

Managing Power, AC and DC

Vital components inside any motorhome manufactured after 1980, specifically those run by electronics, are exposed to sudden termination by a low-power situation. RV parks of all types, whether commercial or private campground, have problems at some point delivering 120 volts to your rig; commonly known as "brownouts."

Purchase a *line monitor* with a digital readout that plugs into an AC outlet. Keep your eye on this meter to gauge the voltage available for use.

Pay particular attention to this reading before turning on the microwave or air conditioning.

Perform regular maintenance on the coach battery bank. Keep the electrolyte level stable as per the manufacturer's recommendations. Some conditioning may be necessary to prolong the life of the batteries.

Consider adding a solar panel with a controller.

Batteries

(See also *Adding Solar Panels*)

Many of the systems in an RV interact and one system can affect the performance of another. There are two different types of battery systems in any Class A or C motorhome.

The *engine battery* is used primarily to start the engine. Some RV manufacturers use this battery to power the radio and cockpit cigarette lighter sockets, other manufacturers use the coach battery system for these features.

It is wise to check the coach documentation and find out how your coach distributes this power system. It is important to keep this battery charged properly.

The engine battery is usually located near the generator or tucked in underneath the front hood like a car battery. It can be a sealed battery as it gets little use.

Coach batteries are a different system that provides DC electricity to the interior of the coach, for example, the overhead vent fans and most of the interior lighting. This system usually consists of two or more deep cycle batteries.

This system is constantly being discharged by any interior demand requiring DC voltage. This system of batteries is usually located under the entrance steps or nearby.

There is still an ongoing debate about the best type of RV coach battery to purchase: Flooded acid (wet cells), gelled acid (gel cells) or AGM (absorbed glass mat).

The quick answer is two deep-cycle 6V flooded acid batteries. *Interstate* is the brand most commonly available (Sears, Wal-Mart) and reasonably priced. Storage space dictates the actual number of batteries; if boondocking often, find more storage space. If not, two 6V batteries are enough. See below for website links that discuss this subject.

Almost all batteries that are supplied with new RVs are flooded-acid batteries unless you are lucky enough to be able to purchase an extremely high-end RV.

Flooded-acid batteries are the most common lead acid battery because they are cheaper and lighter in weight. Small motorhomes (25-30 feet) work perfectly fine on this type.

Estimate the amount of boondocking (no outside power source) on your itinerary.

If you plan to add solar panels, check to see how much room is available in the outside basement or under the entrance steps in the motorhome to store and hook up these batteries. (See *Adding Solar Panels*)

Replacing a group 24 battery with a group 27 that is physically larger, provides more power over a longer period of time. Check the top of your coach battery for a "group" number imprint.

Tip: If replacing the batteries ensure that the battery box is rinsed or scrubbed clean before installing the new batteries. If acid ash is present, it continues to eat through the metal box after the faulty batteries are replaced.

Insist that the person replacing the batteries wait until the box is clean before inserting the new batteries.

Note: Before deciding how many batteries are needed, keep in mind that the microwave convection oven and the toaster oven do not generally operate without a good park electrical power source or a generator.

Here are a few website links that provide detailed information to help you make a choice.

- www.rv-batteries.com/about.php
- blog.woodalls.com/2010/03/rv-batteries-099-by-professor95/
- www.smithae.com/rv.html

Inverter

Inverters are electronic devices that convert battery power into a form that mimics conventional grid power. Most models produce a "modified square wave."

Premium inverters produce a "pure sine wave" to imitate grid power. This eliminates background noise so that all appliances, including electronics, work without problems.

They are particularly suited for sensitive electronics found in some desktop computers and high-quality sound equipment. This type of inverter is expensive, so most of us use the "modified wave" type.

The inverter in your RV basically does three jobs,:

- Converts the battery power (DC) to AC when not plugged into a park power pedestal.

- Directs DC power to the coach.

- Charges the batteries to keep the them charged properly, no overcharge or undercharge.

All newer Class A coaches should come equipped with an inverter/charger. Check this before purchasing any motorhome, particularly a Class C. Adding an inverter is an expensive labor project, as it must be directly wired into the system. The part cost of a 1000 W inverter is about $400.

Even with a small solar panel, the 1000-Watt size inverter is the best choice for a motorhome under 30 feet.

Keep in mind that the microwave/convection oven and toaster oven do not run on battery power only, so when boondocking these appliances are not available anyway.

Two ways to run the inverter:

▶ Leave the inverter on all the time and use it as a power backup when electrical glitches in the RV park system cause a brief shutdown. It also keeps the batteries charged at the proper rate, no overcharge or undercharge.

▶ Turn it on only when boondocking. In this case, you also need an independent charger to keep the batteries topped off. Running the engine or generator also works as a charger.

Here is a website link for detailed information.

www.doityourselfrv.com/

Scroll to the bottom of the page and type inverter in the search field.

Necessary Accessory

Power Manager

Solve the low-power problem you find in older RV parks by purchasing a power manager, *PowerMaster* (recommended) or *Hughes Autoformer*.

This heavy weatherproof metal box is designed to protect your RV equipment from damage caused by low power called "brownouts" (see below).

Not just a power transformer, these units are designed to take any voltage spike and protect your motorhome's power systems. If the spike is powerful enough these units burn out instead of the appliances (microwave, air conditioner).

Each manufacturer has a return plan in place should that burnout event occur.

From the *Power Master* and *Autoformer* manufacturer's website: *"The unit does not take power from the park. It does not affect the park or input voltage, or make electricity.*

What it is doing is changing the voltage - amperage relationship, lowering the amperage and raising the voltage. Since appliances run better on higher voltage, lower amperage, less overall power is used from the park, and better service is enjoyed from your RV.

A unit running at full output (50 amps) uses 1 amp, but causes appliances to cycle more often and run cooler. This uses less total power from the park."

- *30 and 50 Amp models are available.*
- *As demand changes, the output is adjusted.*
- *Run air conditioning and more of your appliances at the same time."*

For more information (and dealer locations):

- **www.PowerMasterRV.com**
- **www.AutoformersDirect.com**

Less expensive RV surge protectors are available, but they shut off the power during low-power situations.

During the summer heat season, this leaves you stranded without air conditioning. With a PowerMaster installed, you can pretty much forget about this problem.

While your neighbors are sweating in the hot sun outside their rigs, you can be cool and comfortable inside.

Generator

A generator supplies your coach with electricity to run all your lights and appliances just as though you were hooked up to an outside electric source.

It draws its fuel from the gas or diesel tank that supplies the engine. Some RVs have a larger propane tank that also supplies the generator along with the furnace, stove and hot water heater.

If you are planning to stay more than two nights in sites without electric hookups *(called boondocking)*, a generator is a necessity.

Some travelers like to stay in out-of-the-way places to enjoy the desert, lakes and beaches that are easily accessible but do not provide utilities. In order to keep your coach and engine batteries charged, run the generator at least once each day.

Before you leave on your first trip, have the generator serviced by a competent RV mechanic. The oil may need to be changed and the filter checked. It may also need to be tuned to run efficiently.

When not using the generator, regular maintenance is required. To keep it running smoothly, ensure that it is run *no less than 30 minutes once a month*. This can be difficult due to the noise and fumes that could irritate other guests in a residential park.

Check with the park office for the appropriate hours to handle this chore. Running the generator during a *rest stop* along your travel path is also a good place to handle this procedure.

Continue this maintenance even when you store your RV more than one month. Adding a fuel conditioner to the gas/diesel tank might help to extend the maintenance beyond the one-month requirement.

What happens if you do not keep up the maintenance? The generator stops working when you need it the most. A costly repair of replacing the carburetor may also ensue.

Tips for a Happy Toilet

Enzymes, liquid cleaner, and various other chemical solutions for the motorhome toilet are available almost anywhere. I personally cannot stand the sickly perfume smell generated by any of these products. Generally they do not work well either.

For the best smelling results (no smell) in the bathroom, keep it simple. do not flush toilet paper, even the expensive RV type. Store the toilet paper in a lidded container nearby.

This keeps paper from fouling the sensors in the black water tank or creating a blockage that is hard to clear. Paper also creates its own smell that takes a long time to break down in the tank.

Best Maintenance Procedure

1 ... Clean the black water tank using a wand that is inserted into the toilet from inside. You can purchase these at any RV store or Wal-Mart.

This cleaning wand is basically a piece of PVC pipe with a flexible hose and rotating blade at the end. The other end has a hose fitting and a shutoff valve. (*See an illustration on the next page.*)

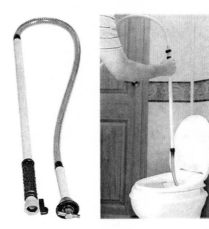

2... Turn off the outside water. Feeding your hose through a window, attach your water hose to this wand and insert it down into the tank. Turn on the outside water and rotate the wand often. It may take 5-10 minutes of fairly high pressure to clean the tank.

To keep from dragging the hose in through a window, a *Water Bandit* can be purchased from any hardware store that slips over the bathroom faucet.

One end of the *Bandit* has a regular male hose end. Attach a five- or ten-foot hose to the wand, turn on the water, and you are in business.

To give you more control over the waterpower, add a shutoff valve to the hose.

3 … After the tank is clean, pour one capful of laundry detergent (scent-free) into the toilet. Allow about 1 minute of water to flow in with the detergent. From now on, follow this procedure after every dump.

4 … Add another capful of detergent before emptying the tank. Without toilet paper clogging the tank, you may only need to dump the black water every two weeks, depending on the size of the tank.

▶ Leave the outside **gray water** tank valve **open** until you see (or smell) the need to drain the black water tank. This eliminates dumping the gray water frequently and prevents backups.

▶ Close the outside gray water valve a couple of days before the black water tank is full. Take a few showers or wash several batches of dishes. It is best to have a rapid gush of gray water to flush the sewer hose properly.

▶ *Important*: Always keep the outside **black water** tank valve **closed** between dumps. Liquid needs to build up to keep the contents from forming hard clumps.

▶ If you smell blowback from the tank, check the outside valve for a leak. Valve replacement may be necessary. Check the park office for a vendor recommendation.

◑ Remember to add one capful of scent-free laundry detergent to the toilet before pulling the outside black water valve.

The electronic sensor lights on the inside control panel are not reliable, so only use them as a heads-up. It seems logical that the sensors located higher in the tank would be more accurate, but depending on the age of the motorhome, be cautious.

If the motorhome is 5 years old or newer, add a capful of liquid (or powder) Calgon Water Softener (Wal-Mart carries this) to the tank along with the laundry detergent. This keeps the sensors free of water deposits and improves sensor accuracy.

Older motorhome tank sensors (depending on the amount of prior maintenance) may not be restored to accuracy by any method except replacement.

Caution: do not forget that the gray water valve is closed just prior to the dump cycle. When you see the shower/tub fill with water from below, it is past time to empty the tanks.

 Important: Never leave the motorhome unattended for any length of time *with the gray water valve closed.*

If you have a Reverse Osmosis water filter system installed (recommended), it continually adds water to the gray water tank until the pressurized storage tank is full. This can add ten gallons or more to the gray water tank

Emptying the Gray and Black Water Tanks

1 ... **Remove the cover from the RV Sewer end. Twist the sewer hose collar** onto the RV sewer pipe. Tug it slightly to test that it is merged securely with the pins on the pipe.

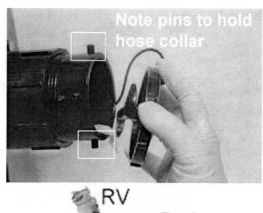

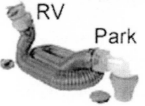

2 ... **Open the black water tank valve.** Wait a few moments to ensure the tank is empty, then **close the valve.**

3 ... **Pull the gray water valve and leave it open.** This allows the black water to be rinsed from the hose to avoid a mess when storing the hose for travel.

Sewer Hose

If you buy a used motorhome it probably already has several sewer hoses and connectors. You may find, however, that they have reached their end-of-life.

RV End

Parking Site Sewer End

When you buy new sewer hoses, purchase a 15-foot *hose* and another 5- or 10-foot extension of the same brand. This hose is made of tougher and more flexible material. This makes storing the hoses easier and takes up less room.

What I especially like about the Valterra Viper shown here is the ease of storing. Even though the material is tough, it collapses down easily.

It has an adapter for the motorhome connection on one end and a seal for the park sewer connection on the other; a clean and neat solution. It is easy to add the extension when necessary.

Purchasing the same brand for both hoses is essential for an easy swap out or extension.

Dragging the sewer hose across gravel or sitting for days on the sharp gravel that most parks use can create small holes. Sharp-beaked birds (usually crows or ravens) seeking water can also penetrate the thinner hoses.

A leaky sewer hose is forbidden in most parks, whether commercial or federal/state run. Not only is it a sanitary issue but varmints are attracted to it as well.

This is a big no-no with state health departments and strictly enforced. Fortunately, I successfully patched my hose temporarily with *Poster Tack* (mentioned above) until I could purchase a new heavy-duty hose.

Sewer Donut

When buying the new sewer hose kit, also pick up a "sewer donut." In most states, you do not need it, but once in a while a certain county regulation requires it.

They are inexpensive. It looks like a rubber donut with one side elongated and narrower than the other side. Squeeze it into any park sewer receptacle and it makes a generic fit for any sewer hose fitting. Some parks do not let you hook up to their sewer without it.

Notes:

Hot Water Heater

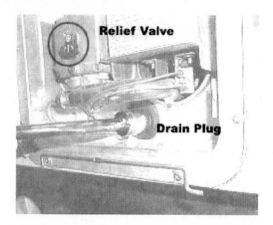

Some motorhomes are equipped with a dual hot water heater, propane and/or electric. Often the hot water heater is fueled by propane only.

With the high price of propane, adding an electric element (Lightning Rod) to the hot water heater may be more efficient. It does take longer for the water to heat up when using only the electric element.

I find that with only one person using the shower and washing the dishes, it is certainly adequate. Adjusting the temperature is easy, turn the dial on the heating element in the outside compartment.

Leaving the temperature set at about 125 degrees seems to work well for me. Set the temperature any higher and the water in the heater tank may start to boil creating scalding water to flow out the faucet.

Nightly and weekly rates at an RV park usually include the cost of electricity. Monthly stays where you pay the electric bill, the lightning rod element does add to the cost.

If you are unfamiliar with or worry about using propane, go all-electric by adding a lightning rod to the hot water heater and purchasing an electric hot plate for the kitchen.

Add an efficient electric spot heater for cool weather to complete the all-electric package. If you decide to go all-electric, turn the propane tank off outside and leave it off. Turn the knob to the right just as if you were turning off water (*see photo - turnoff valve inside circle*).

Propane does not degrade or create a hazard when sitting unused. The tank can be turned on again if necessary without calling a repairperson to make adjustments.

Remember, during *pre-purchase inspection*, ensure that the propane system is checked for leaks. If this important item did not wind up on the list, check it now for later use when you may need propane to run the furnace in sub-zero temperatures or cold rainy days.

Filtering Your Water

Almost every location in the USA suffers from polluted water. To stay healthy, *filter all water coming into* the motorhome. Exterior water filter systems feature a sturdy canister with a filter to take out the heavy materials.

A carbon filter canister can be daisy-chained to the primary filter by using a brass male-to-male or female-to-female hose adapter. These canisters are then connected to your drinking water hose that fastens to the main park water source.

These filters do not remove anything but sediment and chlorine (if using the carbon filter too). *Camping World* and other RV supply stores keep these in stock.

For drinking water, install a Reverse Osmosis water filter system under your kitchen sink cabinet, or under the dinette seat.

The Reverse Osmosis process eliminates bacteria, fluoride, and chlorine.

Of several RO designs available, I recommend a two-gallon storage tank with a four-filter system: carbon, pre-filter, osmosis unit, and the small final filter to take out any storage tank taste or smell. These systems can be ordered online or through a local water store.

Most park-recommended vendors, a local water store, or you can do installation. It is a simple procedure; you just need to ensure that the hoses are connected properly. No AC or DC power required.

It does require at least 40-psi water pressure (the standard for most RV parks). You can purchase a water pressure hose gauge at your local hardware store, or online, if you have reason to doubt the park pressure level.

For complete information on how reverse-osmosis systems work, visit:

science.howstuffworks.com/reverse-osmosis.htm

Hot Weather Tips

Refrigerator

If your travel plans include an extended stay in a hot climate (over 90 degrees F daily), the refrigerator may not stay cool enough to keep food fresh. Installing a couple of 12-volt computer case fans at the top of the refrigerator vent helps eliminate this problem.

Depending on the size of your motorhome, there may only be room for one large fan.

Some refrigerator designs may require the fan to be installed at the bottom. Avoid this if possible.

Some installers may spin a tale about the best installation, but I have tried both top and bottom vent installs and find the fans installed in the top of the vent by far outperforms the bottom location.

The top vent design is a tougher install project and may cost a few more dollars in labor, but well worth it when the temperature hits 110 degrees.

Purchase these small computer case fans yourself at a local electronics/computer store or online (about $5 each), then contact a local RV repair person to install the fans at your RV park site.

Ensure that an on/off switch is also installed for flexibility in colder climates.

✔ Caution: Do not allow the installer to purchase the fans. They do not usually have the correct specifications or understand the reasoning behind using computer case fans over conventional refrigerator vent fans.

✔ Computer fans are also much less expensive at $5 versus refrigerator fans at $35.

Fan Specifications:

Minimum specifications to ensure high airflow and low fan noise:

120mm Computer Case Fan (5 inch): Air Flow (FM) 44.03; Max. Noise dBA) 23.5

80mm Computer Case Fan (3 inch): Air Flow (CFM) 28.89; Max Noise (dBA) 20.9

Inside Wood Cabinets

During hot weather, leave the cabinet doors ajar to ensure ventilation and reduce warping with temperature change.

Window Shields

To maintain cooler temperatures inside the motorhome, purchase sun shades for all the windows.

Although exterior sunshades are somewhat more efficient, they are expensive, difficult and time-consuming to attach and store. You must climb a ladder to put them on and the install requires more strength than most of us have to stretch them across the windshield.

Try RV large spring-loaded shades for the windshield and cockpit windows as they snap closed and store anywhere. Orangewood RV Parts in Phoenix, AZ carries them and they ship. Contact them at (523) 974-3000. Silver Mylar fabric is best but nylon may be all that is available.

Blackout curtains are available at most large truck stops. These curtains have hooks that fit over the top of the main salon or bedroom window valances, the perfect length for a motorhome. You can also have custom-made black shades or curtains created in most small towns and larger metros.

N otes:

Essential Tools

Interior Hand Vacuum Cleaner

Having a cordless hand-held vacuum for the little jobs makes life much more pleasant. There are so many small spaces and corners in a motorhome.

The perfect vacuum for these jobs a **Black & Decker DustBuster Pivot Vacuum 18 V**. This little white giant really has the power. It only runs about 20 minutes on a charge, but can be used around the kitchen, bathroom, and on carpet. It can be stored about anywhere.

Since normally we store any upright or canister vacuum in the lower outside compartments, it becomes a hassle to drag it out for small pickups. This new product by B&D handles little chores perfectly. Most large department stores handle this product, including Target and Wal-Mart.

Velcro Tape

Industrial-strength Velcro can be purchased in rolls and cut to size. Use this versatile tape to anchor the TV, stereo, and other heavy objects that do not have to be moved when traveling. Restrict the use of this tape to surfaces that cannot be marred when the tape is removed. Do not use Velcro for temporary items that might be rearranged later.

Poster Tack or Putty

This soft pliable putty-like substance brings fond memories of our children's play days. Use this to anchor small objects like nick-naks, counter towel holders, hand lotion bottles, and other small items.

The more objects that can be anchored the better. This reduces setup and takedown time while traveling. It takes me about 30 minutes to be travel-ready, primarily because I do not have to schedule time to store all the small items.

Common Household Items

Baking Soda - Pack a couple of small boxes of baking soda for multiple uses around the kitchen and bathroom. Use it to clean the stainless steel sink while also super cleaning the drains.

Liquid Wrench (or similar) silicone spray (not the dry type) is safe to use for squeaky hinges on inside cabinet doors. Vibration from traveling and dry desert air creates lots of opportunities to use this product.

▶ Keep a can of **White Lithium Grease spray** around for long-lasting, heavy-duty lubrication for outside use.

▶ *Touch of Oranges Wood Cleaner & Reconditioner* (or similar product) should be used when you first purchase the motorhome and then every six months to keep your lovely wood cabinets looking good. After cleaning, use a wax of the same brand to protect and bring the wood back to life.

Note: I like the *Touch of Oranges* brand because of the smell; it does a beautiful job, and leaves little residue.

Keep in mind that in a small, enclosed place like a motorhome, the after-smell becomes an important factor when purchasing products.

The common restoration and wax products found in the supermarket often take days before the smell dissipates. A product containing linseed oil has a particular odorous and long-lasting smell.

On the subject of smells, know that *contact adhesive*, often used when replacing headliner material, has a smell that lingers for about three months. It is so strong that you should be prepared to spend time elsewhere for the first month or so.

▶ *Folex Instant Carpet Spot Remover* makes cleaning up those spots quick and easy. Most supermarkets carry this product and it works perfectly.

Extra Cable

Bring 15 to 25 feet of extra RG6 cable as an extension for your high-definition flat-screen TV. It pays to be flexible. Some RV parks may place their cable receptacle in hard to reach locations, so be prepared.

If you plan to carry a portable high-definition satellite TV dish with you, the extra cable may be necessary. Include a couple of barrel connectors (small round adapters that connect two coaxial F connectors together) in this kit.

You may find that the older internal coaxial cable, usually RG59 that runs the length of the coach and terminates at the back of the coach, does not make a good connection to your new high-definition flat screen TV.

Replace it using your RG6 cable from the park cable post through a window directly to the back of the TV.

Ensure that the pins within the F connectors at each end are inserted properly and tight before moving to another solution. It is wise to carry a crimping tool and some extra coaxial F connectors so you can fix your own cable problems.

Replacing all the old original RG59 cable inside the RV with RG6 is an expensive project but it can be done. This is a job for professionals, though, so do your research to find a specialized repair facility.

Drinking Water Hose and Connectors

Drinking
Water Hose
5/8 inch

Male-to-Male Adapter   Female-to-Female Adapter

5/8 x 25 feet
5/8 x 10 feet
5/8 x 04 feet

Carry a male-to-male and a female-to-female drinking water hose adapter in the outside compartment where you keep the water hoses. Put them in the bin where your 4-foot, 10-foot, and 25-foot drinking water hoses are kept.

Some park water connections are not standard, so be prepared. Include a small supply of different size hose gaskets to handle the hose connection leaks that occur without warning.

Include a spray nozzle for washing vehicles and cleaning patios. Make that two spray nozzles, as one is always disabled or leaking.

If you boondock frequently, add a discreet brown or mottled color 15-foot hose for disposing of gray water when appropriate. This color-coding prevents a mix-up with the white fresh water hoses. Carry a "Blue Boy" portable tank as well.

Repair Tools

Organize a small tool kit for odd jobs. Include:

- pair of pliers
- pair of needle nose pliers
- small hammer
- rubber mallet
- package of assorted metal and wood screws
- screwdriver or two (flat and Phillips heads)
- wrench for plumbing use
- plumbers tape
- small stiff brush for cleaning
- pair of gloves that are flexible but tough

If you are towing a car, be prepared to have a problem now and then detaching the car from the tow bar. Best practice is to unhook on a flat straight surface.

If you decide to unhook the toad while the motorhome is at an odd angle, the safety pins on the tow bar may jam.

I keep a 12-inch spike in my toolkit to dislodge the pins with my rubber mallet. The mallet comes in handy for any number of rescue missions.

Outside Electric Cable Adapter

Motorhomes are designed to either run on a 30-amp or a 50-amp electrical service.

In one of the storage compartments outside is the electrical bay. Inside is a long thick cable that is wired into the motorhome that provides all the A/C electrical connections on the inside.

This cable is plugged into the A/C power pedestal provided by the RV park.

 A 50-amp cable is thick and heavy to lug around. Its plug has three prongs and a rounded ground prong.

 A 30-amp cable is much thinner and lighter with two prongs and a rounded ground prong. Remember, 2 prongs vs. 3.

For a more technical explanation, visit this link:

rvbasics.com/techtips/50-to-30-amp-adapter.html

This AC connection provides current to the air conditioner, microwave, all electrical outlets, and some overhead interior lights.

All but some very old RV parks provide 30-amp service on a AC power pedestal somewhere on the site. 50-amp service is a relatively new upgrade for most parks and an extra service charge usually applies.

Some of the newer parks offer only 50-amp service. Others offer 30-amp and 50-amp service from the same post.

If the motorhome runs on 50-amp, then a 50- to 30-amp adapter is necessary since most overnight stays between destinations may be in older parks. Purchase an adapter that has a small length of cable between each end for ease of use.

Plug the female end to your RV electrical cable, the male end to the power pedestal in the park.

30- to 50-Amp Adapter

If your motorhome is wired for 30-Amp service, use a 30-to-50 Amp adapter to be able to hook up to a 50-Amp power pedestal.

Simply plug in the female end of the adapter to your RV electrical cable and the male end to the 50-Amp power pedestal on your site.

This **does not** give the motorhome 50-Amp service, but it does improve the quality of the voltage used inside.

50- to 30-Amp Adapter

This 50-to-30 Amp adapter is used if your RV is wired for

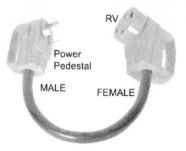

50-Amp service but the only option on the power pedestal is 30 amps.

Pay close attention to the voltage meter inside, as you cannot run both air conditioners on 30-Amp service.

N otes:

Towing Your Car

To tow or not to tow is a major decision for most motorhome travelers. Take your first short trip without a tow in place, then make the decision.

The cost of fuel, the inconvenience of hooking and unhooking the tow, the lack of transportation at your destination, and road safety are the factors usually discussed on this issue.

Not towing any vehicle behind the RV

Upside:

▶ More flexibility for the driver

▶ No increased fuel cost

Downside:

▶ Hassle of finding a rental auto while at destination

▶ Limits exploration due to the lack of convenient transportation

▶*Without a tow car,* it is possible to hire someone in the RV park to shuttle you to the grocery store. However, if you like to explore museums and tourist attractions, this might get cumbersome.

▶In you are in a metro area, hiring a taxi is a viable option. Some parks actually have cars for hire.

Towing a Vehicle Behind the RV

▶The tow equipment on the back of the motorhome is heavy to lift when adjusting but not outside most women's capabilities.

▶Hooking up and unhooking takes time but most travelers find, it is worth the inconvenience to have the car for touring around the area.

▶You can then attach one of those cute little signs in the rear window of the car, *"I'm a Toad,"* or *"I'm Pushing As Fast As I Can,"* and other fun slogans.

▶Ensure that your "toad" can travel "wheels-down." Wheels-down means that all four wheels touch the road while towing. Not every automobile can be towed wheels-down. Do your research on this. Your current auto may not be capable of being towed in this manner.

▶All you need to do is install a tow rig on the back of your motorhome, and install a receptacle on your car. The expense can be around $1,000 for both vehicles.

▶Some used motorhomes come with the included. Autos can also be purchased as "toads." Try **Craigslist.org** (classified

Car dollies are not recommended. These are hard to man-age, heavy to move by hand and store once at the destination park.

Here are some websites to explore for information:

www.trailerlife.com (lists of towable automobiles)

www.rvnetwork.com/ This is the Escapees forum. Look in the *For Sale* section.

www.**blueox.us**/instruction/**towingbasics101**.htm

Remember to pay close attention to the auto weight as well as the towability.

If purchasing a high-powered diesel motorhome you can pull about any weight. On the other hand, a small gas-powered motorhome has severe limitations on its pulling power. Try to stay under 4,000 pounds if possible.

Obviously going up and down hills or mountains can create a severe strain on the engine, hence the lighter weight. You may also need additional braking power to the tow.

Any tow vehicle is going to get some exterior damage from rocks and debris. When traveling, I use a padded vinyl front cover for my Honda CR-V.

It extends above the windshield and fastens to the doors and wheel wells. It is time consuming to install and store so I do not usually expend the effort for short trips.

When towing, be prepared to have a problem now and then detaching the car from the tow bar. Best practice is to unhook on a flat straight surface.

If you decide to unhook the toad while the motorhome is at an odd angle, the safety pins on the tow bar may jam. I keep a 12-inch spike in my toolkit to dislodge the pins using my rubber mallet.

Motorhome Tires

Since you are going to take the motorhome in for service before you start on your first trip, ask the technician to check the tire pressure and note any bumps, checks, or slits in all four/six tires. Have the technician find the "tire date" for you. Write this down for future reference.

Michelin recommends "any tires in service 10 years or more from the date of manufacture, including spare tires, be replaced with new tires as a simple precaution even if such tires appear serviceable and even if they have not reached the legal wear limit.

> If the cracks are less than 1/32" deep, the tire is O.K. to run.
> Between 1/32" and 2/32", the tire is suspect and should be examined by your tire dealer.
> If the cracks are over 2/32", the tire should be replaced immediately; find the nearest tire store."

Keeping proper tire pressure is one of best ways to help tires last longer. Follow the psi pressure listed on the tire itself. If it is not listed, try looking at the backside of the tires for a *Max Tire Pressure* and do not exceed this.

The pressure listed on the tire is a maximum psi that should not be exceeded at maximum load.

Recommended tire pressure is also displayed on the manufacturer's plaque on the driver side panel, or on inside the glove box door.

My experience is, however, that the psi recommended by the RV manufacturer is too low. It is better to find the psi listed on the tire and follow that recommendation.

After cleaning the motorhome tires with soap and water, apply a carbon black product like 303 Aerospace Protectant. As far as I know, this is the only product that works as advertised in combating UV damage.

⊙ Caution: Any tire dressing that contains petroleum products, alcohol, and/or silicone materials may further damage the tire due to a possible chemical reaction with the antioxidant material in the tire.

Tire Covers

Most owners cover the tires when spending more than a few days in one location. Vinyl covers available at any RV store. However, it is a dirty job to cover and uncover the tires as the vinyl tends to pick up dirt and insects just like the tires. They can also blow off in heavy winds.

The latest tire cover trend is shade cloth. The most effective way is to have snap or twist fasteners permanently installed around the wheel wells. It is easy to remove and store the shade.

Take a look at this vendor's product to fully understand how it works, then find a local vendor to install the shades:

www.sunguard.com/tiresavers.html

Where to Park Your RV

Finding the Best RV Accommodations

Usually the first thing people do when beginning the RV lifestyle is to plan whirlwind trips. Returning home exhausted is not rejuvenating. Unless you take many pictures quickly, you may not remember the trip (see *Trip Diary*).

After a few trips like this, the light dawns; why not pick a destination within 500 miles of home and spend at least one week to enjoy the area? Why not make that first destination a driving school? (*see Driving Schools and Boot Camps* at **RVLifestyleExperts.com.**)

> Stay loose - do not overplan - be opportunistic.
>
> Keep in mind that a "no show" fee runs as high as one night's site fee.
>
> Many State parks require reservations and may turn away drive-ups.
>
> Commercial parks sometimes require the first night to be paid in advance, but drive-ups are never turned away if space is available.
>
> Membership parks usually accept drive-ups for at least one night, but reservations are encouraged so plan ahead.

There are several national RV directories available in print. Keep one of these onboard, just in case you cannot get a signal on your phone to access the online versions.

Trip Diary

It may be necessary to create a trip diary to keep a proper perspective on life.

☑ Jot down the date, cost of overnight stay, length of stay and park rating for the next visit.

☑ Use a 1 to 5 rating, with 5 as the best experience.

☑ Make a note if full hookups are not available. Include any discounts available and what card is accepted.

☑ Include information on views, modem friendliness, satellite access, and amenities provided.

Discount Park Memberships

For short stays between destination parks, purchase a discount campground directory. These discount club memberships cost $50 to $80 per year and provide a 10% to 50% discount off nightly rates. The one-year membership fee can be earned back with only two nights at a discounted commercial park.

Restrictions apply to holidays and peak seasonal use. Length of discounted stay is often limited to one week (or one night) depending on individual park rules. These memberships are great for short stays on the way to your destination park.

The parks listed are commercial parks. Usually they are located far off the major highway route, but sometimes they are just huge parks trying to fill their sites.

The printed and online directories included with each membership include directions to each park, the cost after the discount, and any restrictions. To the discounted price listed in the directory, add local taxes and park fees.

Best practice is to call the park first to make reservations and to ensure the discount is still applicable along with the final cost. Sometimes the extra charges cancel out the discount. Listed here are the most popular discount cards:

- Passport America, *www.campsave50percent.com* (50% discount)
- Happy Camper, *www.camphalfprice.com* (50% discount)
- Enjoy America, *enjoyamerica.com* (50% off first night)
- Good Sam Club, *www.goodsam.com* (10% discount)
- Escapees, *www.escapees.com* (15%-50% discount)
- For reliable park reviews, visit **RVParkReviews.com**.

If your planned stay exceeds one or two nights, "google" the park before making the reservation call.

Private campground Systems

Each private campground *system* membership consists of parks located around the USA and Canada that provide scheduled activities, special events, swimming pools, golf courses, casino tours, and good security.

Private campground *systems* usually charge an one-time membership fee plus annual maintenance, similar to an HOA for homeowners. You do not own the RV site but pay for the privilege of using one space for a few days or a few weeks during each stay.

The maintenance fee entitles you to a set amount of free visits. A standard contract allows you to spend two weeks in the park and be out of their system for one week before returning for another two-week stay. Some contracts allow you to spend that "out" week in another park in the same park system.

A binding contract ensures the payment of the maintenance fee for normally three to ten years. This contract can be re-sold at any time if you decide to stop traveling and want to stop paying the maintenance fee before the contract expires. These are called "resales."

Generally, after the contract expires the maintenance fee (and use of the park) continues until you cancel. There is no need to purchase a "lifetime" contract.

Some parks also offer year-round site availability for an extra fee but restrict your visits to a six-month period to keep their RV campground status for local and state tax purposes. One site is assigned for your use anytime within that six-month period. Expect to pay an additional $2,500 to $5,500 a year depending on the park location.

Most park systems also have seasonal rates by the month, cheaper if you commit to three to six months up front.

Each private campground *system* offers the opportunity to purchase an annual membership in a private campground network ($60-$140 annually) that consists of hundreds of private parks that open their resorts to you without an individual park system membership.

Hundreds of quality RV parks across the nation become available for a low nightly cost.

Listed here are a few websites to visit. Keep in mind that the financial status of each system should be researched before purchasing a membership.

The campground websites listed here are *not* "time-share" entities but corporate-owned and maintained with no structured access limitations other than those dictated in the purchase contract.

List of Private Campground Systems

Thousand Trails *www.thousandtrails.com*
(recommended - 52+ parks in USA and Canada)

Sunrise Resorts *www.sunriseresorts.com*
(12 parks - Alaska, Washington, Nevada, Arizona)

Colorado River Adventures
www.coloradoriveradventures.com
(10 parks - California, Arizona)

K/M Resorts *www.kmresorts.com/*
(8 parks - Washington only)

Outdoor Adventures *www.outdooradventuresinc.com/*
(5 parks - Michigan only)

Caution: Avoid "time-share" resorts such as Advance Resorts of America.

Private Campground Networks

These memberships are purchased through your park campground **system** membership. Several different levels of membership are available so ask about all options. These networks offer hundreds of private parks around the country that open their doors to you for a few nights or a few weeks without an individual park membership.

Networks are a cooperative venture supported by private park *systems* to introduce you to their particular park system; no promotional seminars or salespeople. Simply make a reservation through your Network reservation system. Check in at the park office and go to your site.

Resorts of Distinction (ROD)

www.resortsofdistinction.com

Parks International (RPI)

resortparks.com

Coast-to-Coast Resorts

coastresorts.com

Adventure Outdoor Resorts (AOR)

www.aorcamping.com/

Advantages of Private Membership

Save Money

Stay at commercial parks and pay the ever increasing rates, or limit that expense to occasional one-night stops by purchasing a private RV campground membership.

- Commercial parks rates range from $22 to $100 per night, depending on the area and season. If you are on the road for 30 days, this becomes a pricey $660 to $3,000.

- Most State park systems, if you can get a reservation, range from $15 to $24 per night, an extra vehicle is $5 additional. These sites rarely offer more than water and electric. You must make reservations in advance.

- The National Park system, such as Yosemite and Yellowstone, contract out their RV facilities to commercial vendors, resulting in $25-$55 rates. This is over and above the $20 park entrance fee.

Better Security

Membership parks usually have at least security gates and/or patrolling teams. Commercial parks are open to the public with little or no security precautions.

Best Way to Purchase

To purchase a private RV campground *system* membership without paying the hefty entry fee, buy a "resale" membership. The best place to find a resale offer is by searching on the Internet.

Private sellers advertise frequently on the Internet, and in RV magazines. Some members who are going off the road simply want to get out from under the annual maintenance fee.

Brokers who resell these memberships can charge anywhere from $99 to $299 for this service, plus the cost of the membership. Research these brokers carefully as scams abound in this market.

Listed here are some websites that display ads from private and broker resellers. Use a search engine, such as *google.com* or *bing.com*, to find additional websites.

- *www.rv-online.com* (classified ads)
- *www.rvproperty.com* (links)
- www.rvproperty.com/memberships/camping-memberships-for-sale/ (classified ads)
- *www.campresorts.com* (Broker)
- *www.rvmemberships.net* (Broker)
- *www.rv.net* (Forum in RV Community)

Checklist for Purchasing a Membership

Before purchasing an private campground membership, check the park system's financial statement and year-end report on the Internet. Park system failure in this industry is well known. Currently the popular park system *Western Horizons* is financially defunct, so it would be wise to avoid this park system. Yes, they are still selling memberships.

Do your homework before surrendering to a fast-talking salesperson during a presentation. Save hundreds, in some cases, thousands of dollars by spending a few hours researching the different memberships available.

- Visit the website that outlines the park system locations and quality of facilities.

- Check the Internet for resales **first** before talking to a park salesperson as often you must sign a disclosure document stating "no contact with the park salesperson for one year" before a resale is processed. Be alert here!

- Make sure there are parks in the areas you plan to roam and stay.

- Ask to see the rule book provided to members. Check the restrictions regarding guests and parking your extra vehicle.

- Note how many parks are available to you and compare the total with other park systems. Often a three-park system charges as much for the membership fee as a 12- or 52-park system. Also compare annual maintenance fees.

✔ Note how much time you must be out of the system before returning or whether you are allowed to move directly to another park within the system.

✔ Compare each membership system benefits to the information you have compiled on various park systems. Find out if guests that stay with you warrant an extra fee. If you travel with an extra vehicle are you charged yet another fee.

✔ Ensure that there are parks where you plan to travel. A bargain price for parks not in your travel path is not a good choice.

✔ If you are starting to travel full-time, the best choice is the system that offers the most parks.

Caution: "Time share" offers are **not** the best deals for RVers as the stay options are limited.

Boondocking (Primitive Parking)

Parking overnight in areas without facilities (water, power, sewer) usually means out in the "boonies," away from city lights and people; hence, the term "boondocking."

Boondocking has expanded to include overnight parking in a paved parking lot, such as a Wal-Mart store, city street, or highway rest stop.

For great money savings, privacy, and gorgeous scenery, boondocking is great. For comfort and peace of mind, boondocking may not be your style. As a woman traveling solo, try caravanning with others, or meeting up with a group of friends until you are familiar with the lifestyle.

Try boondocking for one or two nights to test your rig's configuration. Do this in the safety of a campground to limit any anxieties or deficiencies. Save a few dollars by requesting the dry camp area. During the peak of the summer season, plenty of opportunities arise to test your equipment and patience.

Essential Boondocking Equipment

If you plan to spend more than two or three nights without AC power from an outside source, add a few necessities to that perfect RV list.

Keep in mind that fifth wheels and trailers often are sold without any of these items. Most Class A motorhomes are equipped with the *Occasionally Boondocking* list. **Some** Class C motorhomes have the short list.

Boondocking as a Lifestyle

- Generator

- Inverter (not converter)

- Extra Battery Capacity

- Solar Panels

- Large Fresh Water, Gray Water, and Black Water Tanks

- Blue Boy portable container to transport black water (when necessary)

- Outside cooking equipment that runs on propane

- Become a devout water conserver

- Become energy efficient with water, computer and lighting use

Occasionally Boondocking

If you only plan to boondock a few times a year at rallies, then spend the rest of the time plugged into power at an RV Park, the list is shorter.

- Generator

- Two deep cycle batteries

- Inverter (to properly charge the batteries and provide A/C backup)

Adding Solar Panels

If the boondocking lifestyle appeals to you, adding a few solar panels to the RV roof can make all the difference. With enough power charging the batteries, all the comforts of home are available to you. According to the experts, the output of batteries and the output of solar panels should match.

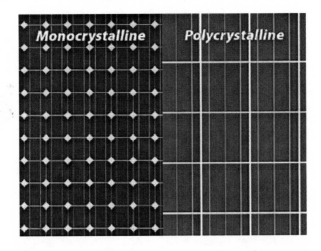

A visit to **AmSolar.com** and the basics facts about solar panels begins to turn into a design plan. They recommend the Crystalline panels for RV roofs.

Types: There are presently three commercially available types of solar cells based on silicon: Amorphous (thin film), Poly-Crystalline (multi-crystal), and Mono-Crystalline (single crystal). Not all types are appropriate for use on RV roofs.

Voltage: The cells have a positive and a negative side. Regardless of the size of the cell, it has a potential voltage of about 0.5 volts.

So, roughly one volt is produced by having two cells in series (2 x 0.5 = 1). In order to develop enough voltage to charge a battery, you need 36 standard Poly or Mono Crystalline cells in series. A 36-cell panel would produce about 18 volts (36 x 0.5 = 18).

Size and Amps: The size of the cell has everything to do with how many charging amps are produced (even if the voltage is not affected by cell size).

The bigger the cell, the more sunlight it can receive, and therefore, the more amperage it produces. It really is that simple. Do your research.

Rating: Panels are rated in Watts of output. This wattage rating is derived by multiplying the panels peak power voltage times its peak power amperage (Watts = Volts x Amps).

Reliability: There is little that can go wrong with a solar panel short of physical damage.

There are no moving parts to wear out and they do not consume any fuel. As long as there is enough light to cast a shadow on the ground, they produce electricity.

Efficiency: Since roof space on an RV is at a premium, efficiency is worth considering.

Efficiency in this situation is defined as: How much of the available energy in sunlight is transformed into usable DC electricity.

In other words: How many of those 1000 watts/square meters coming from the sun are available to you.

- Amorphous panels are about 6 to 8% efficient.

- Screen Printed Poly-Crystalline panels are about 14 to 16% efficient.

- Screen Printed Mono-Crystalline panels are about 15 to 17% efficient.

- GS100 Back Contact Mono-Crystalline panels are about 18.3% efficient.

This technology changes often, so do your research on the Internet for any new developments in the solar field.

Inverter

Converters do absolutely nothing for you when boondocked. A converter converts AC power to DC power. If you are not plugged in, you have no AC power to convert.

Inverters convert DC power to AC power, allowing you to run equipment off your batteries that you would otherwise need to be plugged in to run.

You want to size your inverter to the maximum load it is used for, especially if you plan to use the microwave.

Keep in mind, a microwave pulls a lot of power out of the battery and you need to get that power back into the battery somehow.

You can also make the decision not to run the microwave when boondocking, this saves money when you total up the list.

If possible, isolate the water heater, air conditioner and refrigerator circuits from the inverter. This equipment has such a large draw on the batteries that they would be drained in no time.

To solve this problem, run the water heater and refrigerator on propane when boondocking.

If the weather is hot enough to turn on the air conditioner, move to cooler location.

Most inverters produce a modified sine wave and run most appliances. Some appliances require a pure sine wave to operate, such as some laser printers and computerized sewing machines. Pure sine wave inverters are available; however, they are more expensive.

Generally, the closer the inverter is sized to the load, the more efficient it is. Experienced boondockers purchase small inverters to run specific tools, therefore making the energy more efficient and controllable.

Batteries

The "right" battery for an RV is still a hotly discussed subject. Pick any forum and join the fray; the opinions range from AGM and Gel to the old favorite, flooded cell. The new option on the market is the Lithium-Ion and it looks like a winner.

Lithium

Lithium batteries on the other hand, are a much more recent invention, and have only been commercially viable since the 1980s. We should start seeing them in high-end motorhomes soon.

As cheaper versions start appearing, look for them as aftermarket choices in most RVs.

Lithium Battery Advantages:

- Extended Lifespan
- More Usable Capacity
- Low Voltage Sag
- High Current Output
- Fast & Simple Charging
- Minimal Maintenance
- Efficient Charge/Discharge
- Temperature Resistance
- Easy Placement

- Weight Reduction
- Tax Incentives

True Deep Cycle

Available in Flooded and AGM styles

This type of battery is commonly used as a "house battery" in an RV to power appliances with stored energy from the solar panels.

Lead-acid batteries are made from a mixture of lead plates and sulfuric acid. This original rechargeable battery type, invented way back in 1859, can explode and start a fire or throw sulfuric acid your way.

They are reliable, available everywhere and reasonably priced. They must be vented, so an outside cabinet separated from other equipment is best.

What is a Deep Cycle? A deep cycle is when you start out with a fully charged battery, use 80% of its rated capacity, and then fully recharge it.

Depending on the type, all batteries have a set amount of deep cycles built in before they need to be replaced.

Solar System Sizing by "Rule of Thumb"

RV Solar System Sizing

If you are unable to go "boondocking" to determine how many amp-hours you consume on the average day, then using the following "Rule of Thumb" works well also:

- Use a minimum 100-watt solar panel for basic battery maintenance on Trailers and Fifth Wheels.

- Use a minimum of 200 watts of solar panels for basic battery maintenance on motorhomes.

- For the more Conservative consumers of electricity: Allow 200 to 300 amp-hours of Battery Storage Capacity and 200 to 300 watts of Solar Panels.

- For the more Liberal consumers of electricity: Allow 400 to 600 amp-hours of Battery Storage Capacity and 400 to 600 watts of Solar Panels.

- For "Hard Core" Boondockers with Mobile Offices: Allow 600 to 800 amp-hours of Battery Storage Capacity and 800 to 1000 watts of Solar Panels.

Bear in mind that you can start with one or two solar panels and add more later if needed.

Boondocking Resources

Adding Solar Panels

rvlifestyleexperts.com/fulltime-rving/Adding-Solar-Panels-Resources.htm

Solar Panel Installation

roadslesstraveled.us/solar-power-rv-boat-installation/

Boondocking Basics

rvlifestyleexperts.com/boondocking/boondocking-basics-1.html

Boondockers Welcome

https://www.boondockerswelcome.com/

This website is a connection between those who want to boondock on private land, and those that have private land to share.

Earning an Income

There are a number of opportunities to glean an income while living the RV lifestyle, even if it is seasonal.

▶ To find the perfect workamping employment, start researching and sending resumes about six months before you plan to start traveling on.

▶ Summer positions are usually filled by March 31 and winters jobs by the end of August. Planning ahead is the key to success in workamping.

▶ Wal-Mart employs seasonal workers and prefers the older generation. Visit Walmart.com for an application.

▶ Camping World hires seasonal employees and is open to transferring you to one of their other stores so you can follow the sun.

▶ Amazon.com hires for the Christmas season and prefers retired RVers.

▶Commercial and resort parks hire seasonal employees in exchange for a small salary and a parking spot with full hookups. Sometimes you can just work in exchange for a site.

▶ Several RV-oriented sales companies hire RVers to travel the country selling community ads to be included in local park maps. There is also other type of sales jobs available.

►National parks hire hundreds of seasonal employees to work as rangers, in the food and gift concessions, and as tour guides. This is the biggest resource in the country.

►Be a campground host for the Bureau of Land Management in exchange for full hookups.

Employment Opportunities

If you would like to earn a little money or a lot, work few hours or many, there are plenty of jobs for travelers. You can work seasonally or all year round. Listed here are the popular sites for employment opportunities.

Just a few tips:

► When applying for a position, ensure that you understand every detail of the job description.

► If possible, get names and E-mail addresses (or telephone numbers) of past employees. Contact each one for a full understanding of your employer before you commit.

► Make sure you know the total numbers of work hours expected in return for your site.

► Ensure that the promised RV site has full hookups before you commit.

► Get everything in writing. Since almost everyone has eMail, have your prospective employer send you all the details. Have them include any possible additional duties.

Here a few websites that provide current job openings for RVers via e-mail.

- Workamper News and Workamper in Canada
  www.workamper.com $$
- Workers On Wheels
  www.work-for-rvers-and-campers.com/ Free

- Cool Works
  www.coolworks.com/resort-jobs/ Free

Notes:

Staying In Touch

Mail Forwarding

Find a good **mail forwarding service** in an area you think of as "home base" and have your credit cards and banking accounts changed to this address before you leave home.

Compare annual service box rates with other services in the home base area or elsewhere, such as the Escapees Mail Service in Livingston, TX.

Compare mail forwarding costs and any other handling charges. Insist on a complete listing of all charges possible before signing up for the service.

Only the brave hearted traveler uses General Delivery to receive mail.

In metro areas, there is usually only one US Postal branch for all General Delivery mail, regardless of the address on the envelope.

Call any local branch and ask for the address of that branch before you set out to pick up your mail.

Pay your bills online and stop the paper chase. Most banks now allow you to elect to receive your statements online only.

Credit card and cell phone companies also have the "online only" option.

Cancel all magazine subscriptions except the "must have" ones. There are services out there to help cancel the junk.

Cancel Catalogs: **CatalogChoice.org**

Cancel Credit Card Offers: **OptOutPrescreen.com**

For step-by-step help getting rid of unwanted mail:

www.eco-novice.com/2011/04/goodbye-junk-mail-step-1.html

Cell Phone Service

Compare your current cell phone service with major providers, such as Verizon - the service most full-time RVers use because of the extensive coverage available. AT&T is a close runner-up.

▶ Save money on mobile phone options by purchasing cell phone time from a national provider, not a local provider.

▶ Purchase an external cell antenna (trucker version) for the fringe areas.

⊕ **WilsonElectronics.com** is the most popular brand. They have several packages for the RVer and trucker.

To stay up-to-date on cell phone and Internet issues, visit **Technomadia.com**. This couple travels full-time in a bus and deals with these issues every day. They are traveling geeks and know their stuff.

Traveling Entertainment

Currently both television and radio are available via satellite. There is a cost for the equipment and a monthly charge for the programming. Special deals abound so search for the best bargain.

Television

There are two mobile satellite TV companies available. They are always running promotions, so check their websites for the latest deals.

Dish Network offers the best customer service and the lowest month service fee.

> The equipment costs around $200 and the program monthly fee ranges from $39 to $60.

> DishNet no longer makes the Distant Network channels available but recommends a third-party vendor. Visit their website for the latest promotion, www.dishnetwork.com.

DirecTV provides basically the same programming as Dish and the fees are a little higher. The equipment is around $200. There are always promotions running to entice you, including free equipment.

Visit their website at www.directv.com.

Satellite Radio

There are two mobile satellite radio companies available, XM and Sirius, now merged. Each company offers a different programming approach. The hardware designs are basically the same but tuned to either XM or Sirius.

Satellite Equipment

Ways to Receive the Satellite Radio Signal Transmissions

- Connect the satellite receiver directly to your onboard radio using an auxiliary port already built into your current auto radio. This cable is included with your satellite radio equipment. Highly recommended.
- Connect using a cassette attachment usually included with your satellite radio purchase. Unfortunately most newer car models have abandoned the cassette player for a CD player, so this option is not available.
- Find an unused channel in your current location that can be used to receive the satellite signal. This changes, of course, as you move down the road.
- Entering metro areas causes the satellite signal to be interrupted as the local station takes over.

Of course, you can always purchase and have installed a satellite radio to replace the RV manufacturer's installation.

Buying a New Onboard Satellite Radio

When you see auto radio ads touting "satellite-ready" that usually means that equipment comes with an "aux port" allowing you to connect the satellite receiver directly to the onboard radio.

- This eliminates having to find a blank station on the dial. These ports can be located in the front or the rear of the auto radio.

- True satellite radio usually is installed by a professional as the satellite receiver is built into the radio and the outside antenna needs to be installed.

- Often buying a satellite monthly subscription from the dealer that installs the radio makes the most economic sense.

- All of the new high-end automobiles now come satellite equipped as a standard feature.

Portable or Stationary Receivers?

Keeping the satellite receiver separate from the RV equipment has several advantages:

- If you change RVs the satellite radio moves with you
- Ability to move the radio from the RV to the toad for short trips and have satellite radio all the time
- Several model and antenna designs to choose from

Installing a true satellite radio to replace the standard onboard one does have some advantages:

- Connection is made directly to the stereo speakers already installed throughout your RV without any static interruption
- No fiddling with reception as the antenna is installed on the roof
- Local stations are available with a push of a button

Programming

Sirius provides the most commercial-free programming. $12.95 per month gets you 60 channels of commercial-free music in virtually every genre and 40 additional channels of the news, sports, and entertainment.

The Sirius equipment cost varies depending on the latest promotion. Visit their website at *www.sirius.com.*

XM Radio provides more programming for young people.

- Promotions are always running for free installation and discounts on equipment.
- XM Equipment costs start at $40. Visit their website at *www.xmradio.com.*

Fun and Games

As the storage space in any RV is limited, here are a few lightweight suggestions to fill in those leisurely hours when you are not dancing, fishing, golfing, and hiking.

- Bocce Ball
- Croquet
- Pool Cues (pool tables are provided in most commercial and resort parks)
- Inflatable swimming toys
- Small magnetic chess and checkers games
- Lots of books as used book stores are easy to find these days to recycle your library
- Pickleball rackets and balls (shown above) Developed by full-time RVers, this popular game is similar to tennis played with a whiffle ball and a ping-pong style paddle on a shorter court.
- Laptop computer and printer

Notes:

Maintaining a Comfortable Lifestyle

Living the Life

Feeling comfortable in your new RV lifestyle is the litmus test for any RVer expecting to spend months or years on the road. Here are a few suggestions that can help to make that happen for you.

- Purchase a RV campground *system* membership. Search on the Internet for "resale" memberships that are a fraction of the cost of a new one.

  Visit **RVLifestyleExperts.com** for complete information on this topic.

- Purchase one of the park *networks* available through this campground membership.

  There memberships are usually $70 to $140 dollars a year and provide a directory to parks all across the USA, Canada and Mexico.

This membership opens the door to hundreds of RV parks that offer discounted prices around the country.

Everything from 5-star luxury parks to minimal sites are discounted providing access to gorgeous prime real estate near lakes, seashores and other scenic places across the country.

▷ Equip your RV with the essentials for comfortable living. This does not have to be expensive, just practical and necessary.

▷ Get rid of "things" that do not belong on the road.

This may take a garage sale or two, or rent a storage locker to temporarily store "things" you cherish. You can then dispose of these at your leisure if you decide to stay on the road.

▷ Ensure that all your RVing equipment works.

▷ Carry the necessary tools to fix plumbing and electrical problems as they arise.

▷ There are lots of "fix-it" books available to help you accomplish this. You do not need experience, just be willing to learn as you go.

▷ If necessary, attend one of the RV schools available. Check the RV rally nearest you.

Visit **RVLifestyleExperts.com** for current information on driving schools and boot camps.

These schools provide courses in driving, RV maintenance, purchasing an RV, solar living, and many other topics. They also weight your rig.

▷ Learn to plan your travel routes with plenty of stops between destinations. Trying to see the USA in one year leads to frustration and exhaustion.

- Plan a leisurely journey that allows you to see one section of the country with all its attractions before moving on to the next.

  Putting the most miles on your rig in one year (or season) is not the goal here.

- With the high cost of fuel, lingering in one place for a few weeks is also a practical approach.

- Spend your maintenance dollars where it counts.

  Ensure that the engine gets its periodic service along with timely filter changes.

  Diesel engines particularly need a close watch to prevent dust and grime from entering the fuel system. Check this filter frequently if in dusty areas.

- RV interiors need to be customized for comfort.

  To live the good life, interior lightning needs to be appropriate, comfortable seating and eating arrangements should suit your needs.

  Do not forget outdoor accessories for those glorious days that abound.

- Most Rvers love to socialize, play cards, gamble, take hikes, play on the water, engage in challenging geocaching forays ...the list goes on.

- Today's RVer is younger, healthier, more physical, and more creative than in the past.

- Create your own adventure trek or join in with others to explore the area.

- There are no limits now as you can travel to an adventure or make one up where you are.

Additional Resources

- CDs and books on RV ratings and what to look for. RV Consumer Group. **www.rv.org**
- How to buy an RV. Free information at: **RVLifestyleExperts.com**
- RV Basics - Specific Maintenance Information. **www.rvbasics.com/**
- Articles and newsletters for the new RVer. **www.newrver.com/**
- Excellent Source for Free Computer Help. **www.rverscomputerhelp.com/**
- RV E-Book Library. **www.rveducation101.com**
- Join RVillage.com, a communication tool
- The author's blog, **MovingOnWithMargo.com**

Follow Margo's blog, MovingOnWithMargo.com

Other Books by Margo Armstrong:

RV LIFESTYLE
* *For Women Only: Traveling Solo In Your RV, The Adventure of a Lifetime*
* *For Women Only: Motorhome Maintenance*
* *How To Save Money While Enjoying The RV Lifestyle*
* *The RV Lifestyle: A Dream Come True*
* *Selling Online - Supporting the Traveling Lifestyle*
* *Staying In Touch, A Traveler's Guide*
* *Working On The Road - For Professionals and Just Fun-Loving Folks*
* *Conquer the Road: RV Maintenance for Travelers*
* *Healthcare and the RV Lifestyle*

TRAVEL
* *Welcome to Las Vegas - The Essential Guide*

WRITING EBOOKS
* *Writing & Publishing eBooks - One Person's Journey*

TOOLS FOR LIVING
* *Get Amazing Photos From Your Point & Shoot Camera*
* *Buying and Selling Gold and Silver - A Primer for the Beginning Investor*
* *Selling Your Home - How the Real Estate Market Works*
* *Do Your Own Probate - Summary Administration for Small Estates*

FOOD FOR THOUGHT
* *What Determines Our Destiny*

WOMEN'S STUDIES
* *Answering the Call - Women in Action, Vol 1: Leaders in the World*
* *Answering the Call - Women in Action, Vol 2: Leaders in America*
* *About Men - Myths Revealed, How to Love, Live, and Work With Them*

For Women Only: Traveling Solo in Your RV

CPSIA information can be obtained
at www.ICGtesting.com
Printed in the USA
LVOW12s0315230418
574500LV00001B/87/P